You Are a
Miracle

YOU ARE A MIRACLE

THIS BOOK WILL CHANGE THE WAY
YOU LOOK AT YOUR LIFE

AUGUSTO CURY

Translation edited by Mark Hanks

metro

Published by Metro Publishing Ltd,
3, Bramber Court, 2 Bramber Road,
London W14 9PB, England

First published in paperback in 2003

ISBN 1 84358 074 8

British Library Cataloguing-in-Publication Data:

A catalogue record for this book is available from the British Library.

Design by Envy

Printed in Great Britain by Creative Print and Design, Wales

1 3 5 7 9 10 8 6 4 2

Text copyright Augusto Cury

Papers used by Metro Publishing are natural, recyclable products made from
wood grown in sustainable forests. The manufacturing processes conform to the
environmental regulations of the country of origin.

Introduction

This book is about the profound love of life that is buried deep in the heart of every human being. It is your, and everybody's, biography. Your life story may not have been written before, but in these pages it is told, at least in part. As you read on you will rediscover that which you can't afford to forget, but mostly you will see for the first time why you are one of life's winners, the bravest among the brave, and you will realise how it is only the madness and beauty of love that can nourish and keep you alive.

Deep down, you are profoundly in love with life. And that love began right back at the simple and miraculous moment when you arrived in this world. Yet life is complex and unpredictable, and as the stresses and strains of living in a harsh world take their toll, that love of life may start to bury itself until we become obscure, even to ourselves. We must dig it back up, and though that retrieval learn to turn even the hardest moments of existence to our advantage and embrace the ever-changing narrative of life.

AUGUSTO CURY
(Psychiatrist, Psychotherapist,
Scientist and Writer)

*You are
irreplaceable*

1

All humans experience the turmoil of need. Difficulties present themselves in many ways to many people – some need more food on the table, others are emotionally impoverished – their hunger is in the soul. Some triumph commercially, yet their wealth cannot buy the nourishment of peace and happiness. What areas do you need to nourish?

2

When man has come to understand the workings of the tiniest atom and the hugeness of infinity; when he has claimed to rule the world, then created technologies greater and more intelligent than himself; when he declares there is nothing left to learn of the physical, it is then he will have time to examine his inner self. Now he will realise his grand mistake. What is that mistake?

3

He will realise that, while he may have mastered the outer world, he has come nowhere near to understanding the inner one. The endless terrain of the soul has been left unexplored, and though he may be a giant in the land of science, he is but a tiny and fragile infant adrift in a vast sea of emotion, lost in the interminable landscape of the soul. Unable to navigate a myriad of spiritual cross-currents, storms and whirlpools, he will be lost to himself.

4

But when this happens there will be a new beginning. Man will once again meet his greatest invention, the wheel. 'The wheel?' you say. Yes, but this time it will be the wheel of emotion. When found, it will enable those territories to be explored and traversed like never before. And at the end of this roaming, he will come face to face what he has always searched for: Love. Love for life and for the Author of life.

5

When he learns to love he will shed tears. Tears not of sadness, but of joy and happiness. War and injustice will not be the cause of his tears. Rather, he will weep at the realisation that he has sought happiness in vain, and that God has hidden it in the one place he never thought to search – inside himself.

6

That day meaning will flood into his life like rain onto parched land. A silent revolution will take place in the depth of his being: pride will be replaced by modesty, judgment by respect, prejudice by acceptance, ignorance and confusion by wisdom. Yet that time is still far away. Why?

7

Because we have not yet understood that misery can only be helped on an emotional level. Man dreams of happy days, yet does not know how find them. Great wars have been fought, and great power sought, in the name of happiness – armies have besieged it, weapons have threatened it. But to no avail – for happiness does not answer to power.

8

Magnates try to buy happiness. They build empires, gather fortunes, and adorn themselves with glittering jewels. Yet happiness eludes them as it is not for sale, and money has no currency in the marketplace of emotion, where beggars live in palaces and the wealthy roam the streets.

9

Scientists seek to understand happiness. Statistics are gathered, data collected, the greatest minds on earth employed. But they are misled, as not even the most magnificent equation in physics or maths can interpret emotion. So therefore the scientist is baffled, and destined to be unfulfilled.

10

Intellectuals pore over weighty books of philosophy in search of it. But they seek in vain. Why? Because there are more mysteries lying between emotion and reason than any mind could ever dream of. So, even though they love the world of ideas, thinkers cannot be truly happy because they dismiss the world of emotion.

11

Famous people attempt to seduce happiness. They court the public and make themselves exclusive and mysterious, seeking the adulation and envy of others. But happiness wants to wake them up, shouting: 'I am hidden in the core of simple things!' The famous cannot hear this, though often their fame is not working for them. The simplicity of life is lost to them and they live in the worst state of loneliness – being lonely amongst the multitude.

12

Young People cry out 'we hold the key to living!' They hold parties and performances; some use drugs and relish living in danger. But happiness shocks them when it says, 'I am not found in immediate pleasure, nor do I reveal myself to those who undervalue the future and care not about the consequences of their actions.'

13

Some believe that they can cultivate happiness through solitude. They isolate themselves from others, shunning the world and its troubles in an attempt to banish the difficulties of life. 'We are trouble free,' they shout. Yet happiness leaves them altogether, saying, 'I thrive on life and all its complications; I grow out of troubles.'

Why have so many of us failed to attract happiness? Because we want to smell the roses without taking the time to tend and grow them; because we want to stand glorious on the podium top but despise the effort of training hard. We must go to work on happiness, and practise sailing the sea of emotions if we want quality of life in this stressful world.

15

There is no place for empty resolutions in the world of emotion. 'From now on I will wake up in a good mood'; 'from now on I will be peaceful'; 'from now on I will be a happy person, in high spirits and filled with high self-esteem' – to misguide oneself like this is a terrible mistake, for what is said at the end of a day is forgotten by the time the next begins.

16

There are two key words in the world of emotion: 'training' and 'education'. You have to train your emotions in order to be happy. You have to educate them so that you can overcome losses, frustrations and disappointments. Without this, your emotions will never be stable or capable of beholding beauty in the small details of daily life. Do you behold beauty?

17

An exceptional master of emotion has walked on this earth. He could raise his eyes and find beauty in environments made of stone and sand. Despite his fame, and the intense opposition he met with, he could stand and say, 'Stop, watch the lilies of the fields.' Only someone thoroughly happy and at ease with themselves can master their thoughts peacefully and turn a small flower into a performance before their eyes.

18

However, many people cannot feel pleasure in living. They are easily discouraged and anxious. Too easily, they conclude that happiness does not exist, that it is an impossible dream. They feel too weak to conquer their negative thoughts and win their daily battles. Some, despite an absence of external problems, have lost their sense of being alive.

19

Life is extremely beautiful, but living
in the garden of life is not always simple.
The landscape can change and suddenly life
is as dry as a desert or as steep as a mountain.
But we must climb, no matter how high the
cliffs are– every human being has incredible
strength, but many are unaware of it.

20

In order to prove this, let me tell you an amazing story. It is about someone who, against all the odds, won an incredible fight for their life. Someone who, on that day, was the greatest winner on earth …

21

You!

22

You were once a competitor in the greatest of all races. Over forty million hopefuls turned up, but there could only be one winner. You were that winner. Think about this, and ask yourself, 'Was it pure luck or was there something special about me?'

23

Just think what your chances were – 0.000000025 – you've never been as close to nothing! All the odds were for your defeat. It was insanity to participate in this race, but you took part, and even thought you would win.

24

It would have been easy to give up and accept defeat. But you were incredibly stubborn; your courage was staggering. This is why you never considered defeat as an option – 'give up' was not a word in your genetic dictionary. Why? Because losing that race would have lost you the greatest prize in the world …

25

LIFE!

26

That's right, you have already taken place in the most exciting and dangerous adventure in existence – the race of millions of sperm to fertilise an egg. It would have been easier to win the lottery ten times over, but you made it! How did you do it? I feel honoured to have you as a reader.

27

'But,' I hear you say, 'Wasn't every human being a winner, though?' Of course, but this is *your* biography – only you are the success of this story. It is your remarkable strength and courage against millions trying to wear you down and step on you that should be celebrated here.

❧

28

Times have changed, though. If somebody tries to step on your toes now, you lose your patience. If you are criticised, you become stressed and insecure. If people are ahead of you in whatever race you find yourself in, you become discouraged and restless. Think back to your roots! Back then, nothing could get you down. You were driven by the dream of being alive, not by your troubles and opponents.

29

You used to be a dreamer. Your genes made you dream of the possibility of life. Do you still dream?

30

In the absence of dreams, life has no sparkle. But without goals, dreams come to nothing. Dreams never come true in the absence of priorities. Dream, establish your goals, your priorities, and then take the risks to make your dreams come true. It is better to try and fail than not to try at all. Remember what a great adventurer you are!

31

Now I will tell you something else that may surprise you. Did you know that you were once the greatest of all mountaineers? How? Let me recount a short story that I am sure will show you …

32

In the spring of 1953 something amazing occurred in Nepal. An international expedition arrived, eagerly aiming to conquer Mount Everest, the top of the world. At 25,650 feet high, it would be a tremendous task. As the group eyed the awesome prospect of snow-capped peaks and rocky mountainside, imagine the fear and excitement taking form in the landscape of their emotions!

33

Two ordinary, unknown, and extremely bold men were part of the expedition – Edmund Hilary and Tenzing Norgay. Casting wisdom aside, they set off with a dream in mind, the pursuit of which would head them toward either glory or chaos. Unless your emotions are consumed by a dream, you stand little chance of fulfilling it.

34

As they pushed on, their bodies grew cold, then colder still until their souls shivered with the fear of avalanche and their lungs cried out for air. Then, at the height of their exhaustion, they reached the mountain top.

Their eyes widened with joy – they had reached the top of the world! Not until they came down form the mountain did the world learn of their incredible feat.

35

Everyone has an ambition to reach the top of something. Some set their sights on fame, some pursue the peaks of professionalism; others climb the ivory tower of academia, whilst for some the acquisition of huge wealth is the only goal. The wiser among us seek the highest quality of life – meaning and understanding, wisdom and peace. Your goal was to get to the top of *life*.

36

Hilary and Norgay's conquest of Everest was an extraordinary and unforgettable moment. Be mindful of their achievement as you ascend towards your peak, and remember that you were once the greatest climber. Your determination was immeasurable. Think how tiny you were, yet how daring! Today you are grown, yet often you feel small. Why is this? Because obstacles intimidate and scare you, sometimes to the point of paralysis.

37

Consider the difference in size between Edmund Hilary and Mount Everest – it is hard to comprehend how tiny he was, yet how far he climbed. Now consider the size of a sperm in relation to the distance you had to travel inside your mother's womb to fertilise the egg. It is even greater, yet nothing stopped you! You have climbed a thousand Everests. Whenever we have a dream, no obstacle is too high to climb.

❧

38

However, there is a chance that the obstacles you face today seem insurmountable. Perhaps you have become an expert in complaining about them, in not facing them head-on. Spending time complaining and worrying about life's frustrations is a waste of energy and will damage your innate love of life. Wake up!

39

Let us look more closely at your endeavour to fertilise the egg and become a human being. Acquainting yourself with the enormous dangers you faced and the action you took is like undergoing a self-esteem workshop. Always remember that, in the beginning, you were not only the greatest mountain climber in history but also the greatest swimmer on earth!

40

You swam towards the egg with no back-up boat, no compass, and no chance to rest. Imagine swimming from Europe to the United States to reach a spot the size of an Easter Egg – and without directions. Your aim would be incredibly accurate. You would break all free swimming records. What's more, this is exactly what you did!

41

For this you should be in the record books. Therefore, never say you have done nothing extraordinary. In the beginning you were a single cell; then you were divided in half, and then in half again. Within a matter of days, you became thousands of cells …

42

Dividing is multiplying in the logic of life. You should follow this logic. You were made in an astonishing and marvellous way inside your mother's womb. All the computers in the world cannot match your complexity. Science is nowhere close to explaining the infinite mystery of your physical being. Never disregard your specialness.

43

You grew inside your mother's womb, wrapped in a luxurious swimming pool of amniotic fluid in which you could move endlessly. Turning around at your will, you kicked your mother a thousand times a day. How disruptive you were, yet how important you felt to your mother.

44

But, lovely as it was, the womb was rather too small a place for your goals to be achieved in. You had to get out into the wide world and prove how much more you had to offer. So, with utter determination you made your way out of the womb. Once again, nothing could stop you. And there you were in the social game.

45

Nowadays you may shun the world, seeking out places of peace and quietude. But back then nobody could keep you in the womb, the most peaceful place of all. You were desperate to announce yourself to the world and, in an amazing moment, you were born. But the world rushed down on you. The light, the noise, the smells were overwhelming.

46

Your instant reaction to this was to scream. This was music to everyone's ears – little did they know that all you wanted to do was return to the safe haven you had just come from. Yet the crying helped you, and you became calm. Crying is the first thing we do in this world, and now we hold back tears in shame. Do not be afraid to cry –even the great do it!

47

For the first few months you could not speak a word, yet everyone talked to you non-stop. But once you could talk and needed someone to really listen, those people shied away and were quiet. This is a pity for it is too easy to become isolated in an emotional world. This is unnatural. Words are all we have, yet so often we do not use them to the full. We must strive to communicate, striking up dialogue with our fellow humans.

48

Sometimes we get it all wrong. When children are born they are cherished at the centre of their parents' worlds. But, little by little, the young are sidelined as the pressures of work take over. Certainly, parents are mostly working for their children, but while they want to give them the world, they too easily forget to give them those hugs and kisses. To a child, the outward signs of love mean more than anything the world has to offer.

49

A child's brain is like a sponge. It absorbs everything, storing countless experiences. Unlike humans, computers must be told what to remember, whereas our memories register information automatically in a beautifully complex and natural process. The phenomenon of A.R.M. (Automatic Register of Memory) gives your intelligence material to work with.

50

Your young mind registered and stored hundreds upon thousands of experiences, thoughts and emotions a day. Formative emotional experiences take priority in your mind; thus fear, love, rejection, and support wove the fabric of your conscious and unconscious memory. Now you must decide which memories to store and which to discard – to do this is to nurture happiness and take care of yourself. Can you take care of yourself?

51

Your mind is an infinite cosmos of stored memories and experiences. Your thoughts turn over in a continuous cycle. Despite the chaotic experience of living, your mind learns to organise itself so that you can enter your memory and, from billions of options, draw out the correct words at any moment. Without you even realising it, you are continually using the building blocks of language to assemble your thoughts. This is a wonderful phenomenon!

52

Think what the chances would be of finding someone in New York or London without knowing their address. It would probably take years. Now think how incredible it is that, within seconds, your can locate information stored in the most most complex of cities – the city of your memory – and use it to generate thousands of ideas each day. Your intelligence works in mysterious ways, yet sometimes you can be your own worst enemy. How paradoxical your mind can be!

53

Once your memory was established, something even more spectacular was born out of it – conscience. A thousand books could not provide an explanation of what it is, yet only by having a conscience can you gain a sense of 'self' and discover what your role is in the theatre of life. Through our sense of self we form relationships, we love, we mourn and we seek to escape the utter solitude of being alive through the divine art of communication.

54

Thus your personality is a multi-layered construct, as delicate as the lightest and most finely constructed of birds' nests, each of your traits shaped and interwoven by your experiences, memories and emotions into a tightly-knitted whole. Some parts of you are brave and strong, others are filled with dreams, yet some aspects of you are negative and lacking in confidence. You cannot delete the memories that make you who you are, but you can still change your personality. How?

55

You can use a special technique called DCD (Doubt, Criticise, and Demand). Doubt anything controlling your emotion that threatens to disrupt your life. Criticise every negative thought – complacency, compliance and passivity must all be questioned and the causes of inner conflict must be considered. Demand happiness, confidence and well being. Broaden your emotional range and embrace new experiences. Be the author, not the victim, of your history!

56

Each and every human being has a role to play on the great stage of humanity. Find yours! Whether rich or poor, and no matter what your colour or creed, you are a unique being and a member of a unique species – the human race! In the search for happiness, we must look beyond our immediate social group and embrace humanity for its wonderful diversity.

57

If you show love for the human race,
you are a revolutionary in the quest for
universal happiness. We may have different
cultures and skills, yet in the ways of the
mind we are all equal. We must seek the
innate and instinctive goodness that lies
within all of us.

58

Any kind of prejudice is insane and inhuman. Just as you should never look down on yourself, you must never place yourself above people. Others may think differently to you, or behave in ways you would not choose to, but to judge is wrong. You must strive to show compassion and understanding towards your fellow humans. It is a wise man who can admit his own mistakes and forgive others theirs.

59

There are two types of wisdom, and one is far superior to the other. The first type is measured by how much a person knows, but the second is gauged by the extent to which a person is conscious of how little he really knows. The first type judges, the second is tolerant. The first type blames, the second forgives. The first considers a university degree as the final measure of knowledge, whereas the second sees us as endless learners. What type of wisdom would you like to have?

60

We all have demons from our pasts. Unless we forgive them, they will never leave us alone. Instead, they will invade the present and limit the future. So how best to face the enemy? Forgive, not through trying to forgive immediately, but rather through understanding your demons first. Once understood, they will be forgiven and will no longer haunt you. Seek your demons and free yourself from them!

61

If people lock doors in front of you and hinder your way, do not waste your strength by pushing and fighting – look for the windows! Consider the natural wisdom of water. Water never fights against what is in its way – it finds another way around. Whenever someone offends or disappoints you, view them as the obstacle and imagine yourself as water. Get around things without argument. Learn to love without expecting too much in return.

62

Protect your feelings. Filter the aggression and intolerance directed at you. Whilst your emotions are the most fragile part of your soul, they are also the most unprotected. A single piece of criticism can destroy your confidence, but only if you let it. If you learn to protect yourself, a thousand insults will wash over you like water off a duck's back.

63

Don't dwell on your failures. Some things are impossible to avoid. When you feel defeated, try to remind yourself of how unlimited our intelligence is – there is often a way out that you just have not found yet. Learn how to plunge the depths of yourself to find it. Be free and lateral in your thinking.

64

But things may not be easy for you now. You self-esteem may be at its lowest ebb, and perhaps you have become frustrated by everything and everyone around you. Well let me tell you about another of the amazing achievements you have made …

65

Do you realise that you have experienced the greatest romance of all? It has already happened to you. When? I will tell you, but first I must tell you something about Shakespeare …

66

The great playwright and poet William Shakespeare let the most passionate feelings and emotions flow into his texts. As he wrote, it was as if he was taking a trip to the extremities of the human soul. He wrote the drama *Romeo and Juliet*, a tragic romance of two lovers prevented from being together. The young and perfect love between these two youths is a beautiful evocation of the infinite depth of human emotion.

67

It could be that Shakespeare based his romance on a couple in Verona, Italy. Indeed, Juliet's house is there, open to visitors. Tourists flock by the thousand every year to feast their eyes on the warm and lovely spectacle of it. Women of every nationality strike poses for photos on the balcony – everybody dreams of pure romance!

❧

68

Have you ever had a great romance? Don't say no! You have lived through the greatest of all romances, and you were loved back too. Your romance was genetic, instinctive and uncontrollable. Hollywood's finest love stories cannot compete with what you have experienced! 'But when did this happen?' I hear you say. Back at the beginning, when you were a lonely little Romeo of a sperm, desperately in love with Juliet, the egg.

69

There were so many obstacles keeping you and your beloved apart. Life could have no meaning until you were united. Only then would you be complete. You did crazy things to keep your love alive.

When you met your Juliet you did not yet have intelligence, only genetic memory and instinct. But, if you had been able to express yourself to her, you would have said something like this: 'I have been trodden on, beaten and squashed; I have climbed mountain after mountain and crossed wide stormy oceans; I have courted danger at every stage in order to get to you. Now I am here I will never leave – you and I will be one forever! Never will I give up on life and I will always love you!'

How bold, strong and true those words are. Yet, as time has passed, it is likely that you're not as in love with life any more. Difficulties present themselves in various ways – your finances make you worry, tiredness and fatigue come knocking at the door unexpected, fear erodes your peace away, and anxious thoughts steal away your happiness. Your smile is no longer as spontaneous and frequent.

72

You may be so busy looking after everyone else and attending to your work that you have no time to attend to yourself. Quality time on your own is important. You must not forget about yourself, nor should you forget the importance of talking to your self – there is nothing wrong with regular doses of introspection. Stop for a while and consider how much attention you really pay yourself. Have you abandoned yourself?

73

You may tidy your house, clean up your desk, organise your files, but this will not help your internal disarray! You need to tidy up your mind, and the way to do this is to switch off, relax. Stop going to the funeral before the death. By this, I mean stop being sad about problems that are yet to occur, and may never occur at all.

74

Modern life is complicated. If your mind is always agitated, your life can become so complicated that confusion and unhappiness take over. This is the most common of modern psychological problems: FTS, or Fast Thinking Syndrome. Whilst this is a real problem, it does not start in the mind. Rather, it begins as a result of lifestyle. What kind of lifestyle do you have?

75

The features of FTS are racing thoughts, fatigue, bad concentration, memory loss and boredom. Mood can change rapidly and, overall, there is a general sense of stress and anxiousness. But the cause of this is simple: over the last hundred years the pace of life has sped up to the point that we are now surrounded by an excess of information – our senses are overloaded and our thoughts cannot keep up.

You may not believe it, but one of the ways your brain protects you from too much information is too switch it off. Your memory starts to fail you, and ill-informed doctors tell you you have mental problems, when in fact your brain is merely trying to save energy and tell you that your life is too hectic.

77

It is likely that, due to FTS, an important part of you has grown old before its time – the emotional part. Is it possible that the one place where you should be free has become imprisoned by itself? Yes? But do not lose heart, because this is not a matter of fate, but of choice. Choose to be free of the emotional shackles that hold you back!

❧

How strange it is that society has never been so advanced and we have never seen such diversity or had so much choice of entertainments, products and services. Education is better than ever, yet at the same time man has never been so sad and vulnerable to mental illness.

79

But never give up. The world may seem crazy, but still you must never allow yourself to be discouraged from living – 'I did not ask to be born' is the excuse you might find for giving up on life. But that is a falsity. Not only did you ask, you *chose* to be born and struggled, *fought* for the right to live. You decided genetically, now you must decide intellectually. Never think about throwing away something you worked so hard to achieve.

80

Always keep in mind that, at the beginning of your story, you were weak, frail and lonely, but you acted like a giant, and with immense bravery too! Now you are amazingly intelligent and talented in so many ways. Also, think about all the people who love and cherish you – you are very important to others. If you think about it, you have so many reasons to overcome your problems and blossom. The fear of pain increases the pain. Face up to it!

81

If you feel that your world is collapsing, that the weight of your problems is unbearable, then I would like you to think about what would have happened had you lost the race for life. Just imagine – you would be free of all your difficulties. There would be no despair, no frustration, no tears.

82

But, on the other hand, you would never have played any role on the stage of life. You would not have felt love, or experienced the joys of friendship and laughter. You would not have had parents to show you kindness, children to cherish, nor troublesome people to teach you life's lessons. You would not have had ears to enjoy the beauty of music, neither would you have eyes to watch the flowers and the trees. Another person would be reading this book.

83

In the face of all this, there is only one thing you can do. Love your life and have the courage to live it out, even if you are sometimes tired and in trouble. Don't forget that man's greatest executioner is man himself. Nobody can hurt you more than you can hurt yourself. Life is beautiful, yet fragile – take care of it!

84

If you are a child, don't try to grow up quickly. If you want to be a happy grown-up, you must first be a happy child. If you want to have fun and be happy, turn the TV off for a while and learn to play, to smile, to run and live with emotional intensity. Adult life is so serious and, with all its anxieties, really isn't something to rush into. Take advantage of your time of innocence. Enjoy your friends, play with your parents and shower people with kisses and touches.

85

If you are a teenager, don't live in a well of dissatisfaction. Do your intelligence justice and learn how to get a lot from a little and to love whatever you have. Value substance over style and treasure the contents rather than the container. Do not look down on your body – rebel against the tyranny of beauty imposed on us by the media and celebrate yourself for what you are. Beauty *is* in the eye of the beholder. Prove that to yourself!

86

If you are an adult, don't act as impulsively as you did when young. Learn to explain, not impose, your ideas. Train to be clear-headed and efficient and practise the art of teamwork. Not that you should live to work. Rather, work to live. Vary your schedule to include activities that promote pleasure and peace. After all, there's no point in being the richest person in the graveyard!

87

If you are elderly, let wisdom take over from intelligence. Do not fear the end of this life, for it is only a drop of water in the great ocean of eternity. Live every minute as if it is a miracle and do not let fear be your master. Retire from work, but do not let your mind retire.

88

We must take advantage of the opportunities life affords us. We must find an oasis in the wilderness. Losers see the lightning and fear destruction, whereas winners see the rain and see it as a chance to water their crops. Losers are obsessed with their losses and failures, but winners look for the opportunity to move on and start again.

89

So I encourage you to be a great entrepreneur. And as you go about your business, be prudent, but do not fear making mistakes. When you do make mistakes, do not be afraid to admit them; and when you admit them, do not be afraid of crying. And when you cry, don't be afraid to rethink your life; and when you rethink it, don't be afraid to give yourself another chance.

90

You were born a winner, and that's exactly what you are today. But being a winner does not mean that you will not make mistakes, that you do not have shortcomings. A huge part of being a success is knowing your limitations and adjusting yourself accordingly. Winning is moving onwards. Always remember that this book is an account of the precious aspects of your biography. You became outstanding the moment the big race started and your life clock started ticking.

91

You were so outstanding that not even an Oscar or Nobel prize, or indeed *any* prize, would have done you justice. But then a divine entity arrived on the scene – God, the Author of existence – about whom we have heard so much yet know so little. He observed you closely, noted your fighting ability and, eventually, he awarded you the greatest of all prizes …

92

THE MIRACLE OF LIFE!

93

Only LIFE could be the prize for the best climber in history, for the greatest swimmer, for the most stubborn person on earth who underwent the greatest romance of all.

94

You are an incredibly strong and special person. Overcoming financial hardship, emotional crises, professional conflict, and even physical illness is nothing compared with the admirable way you conquered turmoil to gain the life that now pulses through you. Never surrender and never give up on those who surround you, no matter whether they disappoint you occasionally.

95

Your age does not matter. Neither does it matter whether you are famous or less well known. It does not matter whether you are undergoing defeat or riding a wave of success. Neither does it matter if, in some situations, you become anxious, tense, desperate or forced to admit that you are wrong.

96

What does matter is that, despite all the obstacles, your life is more beautiful and infinitely complex than the stars in the sky. Your life is the greatest show on earth – the Creator's masterpiece.

97

In the light of your magnificent biography, I ask you to continue fighting for your dreams and hope that you fall more and more in love with life, caring deeply for those close to you, making new friends and making yourself a wonderful and useful contributor to society.

98

Always remember that, though you line up in banks, queue in traffic and stand in line at supermarkets, you are so much more than a face in the crowd or a number on a credit card.

❧

99

You have your shortcomings and anxieties, and of course you make mistakes, but there is no one else like you. Without your unique existence, the universe would not be the same.

100

Think of the facts I have told you in your biography, and never forget that Author of life and all the people who have met you consider you to be one thing ...

101

AN IRREPLACEABLE
HUMAN BEING!